The Game of Mah Jong Illustrated

Patricia A. Thompson and Betty Maloney

'You win some, you lose some' — *Anon.*

Kangaroo Press

Acknowledgements

The authors wish to thank the following friends who have assisted by so willingly lending their Mah Jong sets and books: Elizabeth Davies, Beth Forman, Noel Gray, Brenda Greenfield, Ros Little, Betty McCormick, Heather McMillan, Ruth Mitchell, Del Neal, Gayl and Colin Stewart and Jean Whitehouse.

Thanks are due to The Tramshed at Narrabeen, also to Beth Kennedy and all the members of The Tramshed Mah Jong Club, for their help and encouragement.

Our very special thanks go to Judith and Bern Gould and to Peter and Reg for their loyal support.

The authors would like to thank Penguin Books (NZ) Limited for permission to reproduce a number of the special hands created by Max Robertson and published in his book *The Game of Mah Jong*, Whitcoulls, 1974. Special hands from this book appear in the section 'Further Variations' (page 51).

© Patricia A. Thompson & Betty Maloney 1990

Reprinted 1991, 1992, 1993, 1994, 1995, 1996, 1997, 1998, 1999 twice, 2000 twice and 2003
First published in 1990 by Kangaroo Press
an imprint of Simon & Schuster (Australia) Pty Limited
20 Barcoo Street, East Roseville NSW 2069
Printed in China through Colorcraft Ltd., Hong Kong

ISBN 0 86417 302 4

Contents

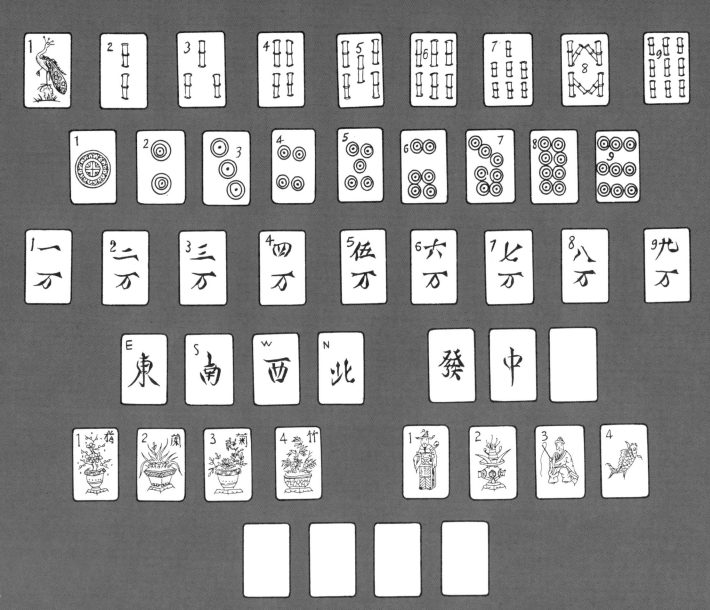

Introduction

Mah Jong is a game for four players (although two, three or five may play) played at a table with a set of 144 tiles.

During the game, the players hold 13 tiles. They play as individuals, not as partners. In turn each player draws one tile at a time from a stack—known as the wall—or picks up a discard, temporarily holding 14 tiles, then puts out one tile.

The objective of the game is to be the first player to obtain either a complete set of four defined groups of three or four tiles and one pair, or certain special hands.

The first player to achieve this structure, which need not bring the highest score, wins the hand.

Because of the absence of partnerships many find the game more attractive than some card games. It leads to less controversy. The tiles are a joy to behold as well as to handle and play becomes more interesting as the nature of the hand changes with each exchange of tiles.

The game still includes many interesting features of the old Chinese game but has been adapted to meet the demands of other countries. A core of enthusiastic American players has introduced limit hands with their own variations.

A problem exists with the interpretation of the rules, which may vary from one expert to another; for clubs and groups a definite set of rules should be established at the start. The advanced player should refer to the specialised books listed in the Bibliography.

The intention of this book is to describe the play, clarify the scoring and give some alternative versions for Mah Jong, so that players may select the game which gives them most pleasure.

The Tiles

The game of Mah Jong is played with a set of 144 small rectangular tiles, the faces of which are decorated with colourful designs. Mah Jong tiles are thought to have developed from dominoes, perhaps by way of a practical change, for the Chinese prefer to stand their tiles in a line with the tiles to be discarded held in the hand. Ivory was used for a brief time but was replaced by bone skilfully dovetailed into a bamboo back. Less expensive sets made of plastic are now available.

To help preserve bamboo tiles and prevent discolouration, it is advisable to place a small piece of camphor with them if they are not contained within a cedar or camphor wood box. Occasional play with the blank tiles will also ensure that all tiles age evenly.

Take good care of your tiles. Do not expose the set to heat, cold or damp; the tiles should be kept clean, especially the backs. Dirt may be removed with a clean dry cloth—water should be avoided. Stains may be removed with a clean cloth moistened in alcohol.

Always treat the tiles with care and respect. A plain cloth on the table will not only protect the tiles but also reduce noise. They should not be tossed, but shuffled by moving the tiles with the finger tips, a few at a time, through the other tiles to the opposite side of the table. Rough treatment may cause minute chips.

If you plan to purchase a set, purchase the best possible; you will not regret it. Unlike playing cards your Mah Jong set will not wear out!

The Set

Number of Tiles

A full set comprises 108 suit tiles, 16 wind tiles, 12 dragon tiles, four flower tiles, and four season tiles, a total of 144, not counting the plain tiles.

The Mah Jong set is divided into three categories:

1. *Suit tiles*—Bamboos, Circles and Characters.
2. *Honour tiles*—Winds, Dragons, and 1s and 9s of each suit.
3. *Flower and Season tiles*—These tiles play no active part in the game, but do affect the final score.

Suits

Each suit is numbered from 1 to 9 inclusive, and there are four tiles for each number (36 × 3 suits = 108 tiles).

The bamboo suit In China the bamboo has always been held in high esteem, being upright, straight, a plant of great versatility and associated with writing. It is evergreen and many of the tiles are green. The 1 Bamboo is decorated with the representation of a bird—sometimes a peacock, denoting dignity and beauty— or a hemp bird. Confusion often arises between the Flower tiles and the 1 Bamboo—remember 'the bird in the bamboo'.

The circle suit Circles, also called 'dots' or 'balls', were originally known as *T'ung*. The dots represented copper coins, and the tiles were engraved with a variety of colour combinations—black, blue, red and green. The 1 Circle has a special significance: to win with this tile is referred to as 'picking the moon from the bottom of the sea', for it is known as 'the Moon of China'.

The character suit Characters, also known as 'cracks', are actually the ten thousands *(wan)* ranging from 10 000 to 90 000. Many of the earlier sets were marked only with the Chinese characters, but now bear the Arabic equivalent. The Character suit is engraved in red and black.

The terminals The 1s and 9s of each suit. They are of more value in scoring than those numbered 2 to 8, and are classed as Honour tiles for scoring purposes.

Plain Tiles

Four extra plain tiles are included as replacements in case tiles are lost.

BAMBOO SUIT

 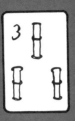 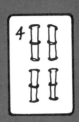   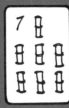 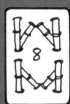 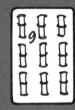

CIRCLE SUIT

  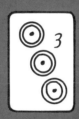 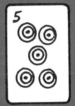 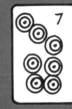 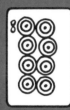 

CHARACTER SUIT

WINDS

| East | South | West | North |

DRAGONS

| Green | Red | White |

WHITE DRAGON VARIATIONS

Wind and Dragon Tiles

The wind tiles   Wind tiles are known as Honour tiles. There are four winds—East, South, West and North. There are four tiles for each wind (4 × 4 = 16 tiles). Each wind is represented by the Chinese symbol and a Roman letter.

The Chinese names for the winds are *tung* (east), *nan* (south), *hsi* (west) and *pei* (north). The word *tung* infers leadership, so the East Wind leads the play. The wind tiles may be used in forming a basic Mah Jong hand either as a pair, three of a kind or four of a kind. Because they are Honour tiles the score is greater.

The dragon tiles   Dragon tiles are also Honour tiles. There are three kinds of Dragons known as Green, Red and White. There are four tiles for each dragon (4 × 3 = 12).

1. Green Dragon tiles are often marked with F *(fa)*, meaning green, the commencement of vegetative life.
2. Red Dragon tiles are sometimes marked with C *(chung)*, centre or middle. This represents animal life.
3. White Dragon tiles often have a frame engraved on them in addition to P *(pai)*, meaning white, pure—representing spiritual beings.

In the original Chinese game these dragon tiles were known simply as Green, Red and White. In fact, they are still often referred to in play as green, red and white. They were subsequently named Dragons by non-Chinese speaking players.

The Dragon tiles may also be used in forming a basic Mah Jong hand either as a pair, or as three or four of a kind. Because they are Honour tiles the score will be greater.

Flower and Season Tiles

The Flower and Season tiles take no part in the play: they simply add a bonus score at the end of the game.

The Flower and Season tiles were originally known as the 'Eight Guardians'—one for each flower and each season. They are the only tiles in the set which are not duplicated. Each Flower and Season belongs to a particular wind:

1. Spring	2. Summer	3. Autumn	4. Winter
1. Plum blossom	2. Orchid	3. Chrysanthemum	4. Bamboo
1. East	2. South	3. West	4. North

If East Wind draws Spring or Plum Blossom, bonus points are awarded because they are East's own flower and season.

The symbols and designs on the Season tiles vary slightly from one set to another, giving each set its own individual appeal. One set may depict occupations, e.g. fisher, woodcutter, farmer, scholar, and another the guardians, e.g. wind, flower, snow and moon. Another set makes architecture its theme. The pinnacle of the engraver's art is represented on the better quality sets.

The Chinese game is rarely played with the Flower and Season tiles as they add an element of luck and allow players a higher score.

When a player draws a Flower tile, it is placed face up on his rack. The player then draws an extra tile from the loose tiles at the end of the wall to regain the correct number of tiles.

The Flower tiles are usually numbered in red and the Season tiles in green, but they do vary from set to set.

Bouquet A set of four Season or four Flower tiles numbered 1–4 is known as a bouquet.

FLOWER TILES

SEASON TILES

9

WIND DISCS

East   South   West   North

DICE

WIND CUBE

COUNTERS

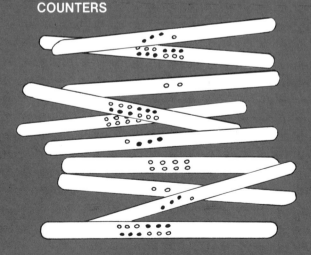

Accessories

Four wind discs   Contained in a box called the *mingg*. They may be used to select seats and to indicate which wind the player represents.

The discs are placed face downwards, shuffled and picked by the players. East Wind selects a seat first.

In the absence of a cube (see below) the discs may be placed in the box with the uppermost disc denoting the Wind of the Round.

Dice   Chinese dice are very small and made to roll easily within the walls. Four or six are included in the dice box although only two are required.

Cube   A cube with the Chinese ideograph for each wind is sometimes included in a set; it is used to indicate the Wind of the Round. It is placed by the player who is the first to be East Wind and changed as necessary.

Counters   These are used for scoring; they have different values, as discussed in the scoring section.

PLAIN OR JOKER TILES

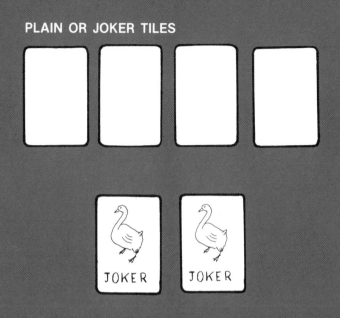

TILE RACK

Plain or Joker Tiles   Some sets contain four Joker tiles. These may be used when playing a Goulash hand (see page 21); otherwise the accepted practice is to use the 2 of the Bamboo suit or the plain tiles.

Racks   A set of racks, popular with Western players, may be purchased with your Mah Jong set. They are used not only for storing the counters and holding the tiles at an angle easily visible to the player, concealed from others, but also to facilitate building the walls. The standard racks usually measure the exact length of the wall (i.e. 18 tiles), making the counting of the tiles during construction unnecessary. Many racks have a flat top for holding exposed tiles. The Chinese generally prefer not to use racks, instead standing their tiles on the table and holding the tiles to be discarded in the hand. In some sets there are three black racks and one red rack, which is used by East Wind.

Design Variations

Tiles vary from set to set. More elaborate designs appear on the more expensive sets.

Engraving on the character suits varies from one set to another as illustrated.

The top two rows of tiles show variations in the 1 Bamboo.
The next two rows demonstrate variations in the Dragon tiles.
Variations in suit tiles are shown in the last two rows.

The Scoring Groups

These are: *Pung*   Three identical tiles
            Kong   Four identical tiles
            Chow   A run of three consecutive tiles in
                         the same suit
            Pair   Two identical tiles

Pung

This is a group of three identical tiles. When a player calls 'Pung' it means, 'Stop the play, I require that discarded tile out of turn so that I can complete a Pung!'

Exposed pung If *any* player requires a tile being discarded to form a Pung (already holding a pair of the same type concealed in his hand), he must call 'Pung' and, laying the two tiles from his hand on his rack, join the discard to them, thus forming an exposed Pung. The required tile must be 'Punged' at the time it is discarded. He must then make a discard, unless going Mah Jong.

Should two players require the same tile, one for a Pung and one for Mah Jong, the player requiring the tile to complete his hand has precedence over the other.

Concealed pung A player may hold a pair concealed in the hand and draw the third tile from the wall to make a Pung—this Pung remains concealed in the hand and is not declared face up. More points are awarded for a concealed Pung than for an exposed

Pung. When revealed at the end of the hand for scoring, the middle tile is turned face down to indicate that the Pung was concealed.

Kong

This is a group of four identical tiles. A Pung may be converted to a Kong in several ways:

Exposed kong 1. Any player holding three identical tiles concealed in his rack when the fourth is discarded may call 'Kong', then expose the three tiles in his hand combined with the discarded tile, all face up. This is known as an exposed Kong. This player *must* take one loose tile, otherwise he is one tile short in number. Always count a Kong as if it consisted of three tiles. **2.** Any player holding three identical tiles previously claimed as a Pung and already exposed on top of the rack, who draws the fourth tile from the wall himself may add it to the exposed Pung to form an exposed Kong. A loose tile must be taken before discarding. A player having an exposed Pung when the fourth is discarded by another player may not claim it to form a Kong.

Concealed kong 1. A player holding three identical tiles concealed in his hand, who draws the fourth from the wall, may lay down the four tiles with the two middle tiles turned face downwards to form a concealed Kong. The player must then take a loose tile before discarding. For each Kong in a completed hand, the hand must contain one extra tile. **2.** Should a player prefer to hold the concealed Kong in hand (maybe to form a Chow with the fourth tile) it will only score as a concealed Pung until declared. (See no. 8 of *Strategies*, page 23.)

Chow (or Chee)

This is a run of three consecutive tiles all in the same suit, e.g. 1, 2, 3 Characters. *Chee* means 'to connect'.

Whether a Chow is concealed or exposed, it scores no points—it merely allows the player to complete the hand with more speed.

Exposed chow Only the player sitting on the right of the discarder may claim a discard to complete a Chow; but a player going Mah Jong has priority over all other claims for the discard. Any player claiming a discard for a Chow must already have in hand two tiles of the Chow, and expose them along with the discarded tile before making a discard.

Concealed chow A player may hold a concealed Chow having drawn all three tiles from the wall. Whether a Chow is exposed or concealed, it has *no* scoring value.

In the Chinese game, any number of Chows are permitted. In the Western game, only one Chow is permitted in the ordinary Mah Jong hand.

Pair

The completed Mah Jong hand must contain a *pair* of identical tiles, known as the 'Sparrow's Head' or 'Pillow', making a total of fourteen tiles.

A pair may be formed from the discard of any other player if it is the last tile required to complete a Mah Jong hand.

Pairs of Dragons, Owners Wind and Wind of the Round score extra points. Points are awarded for completing the pair to go Mah Jong.

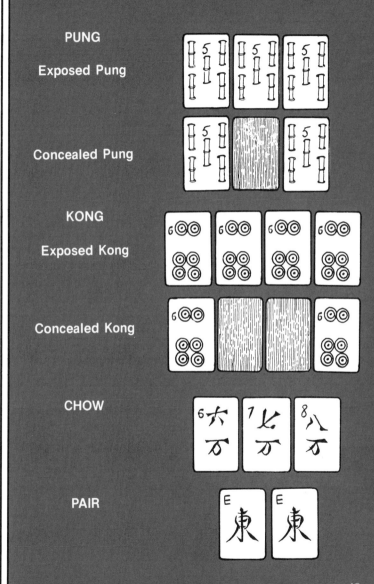

PUNG
Exposed Pung

Concealed Pung

KONG
Exposed Kong

Concealed Kong

CHOW

PAIR

Background to the Game

Chinese philosophy and culture, developed over the centuries since long before the dawning of Christianity, have contributed to the game of Mah Jong. The counters, dice and wind discs have been portrayed as far back as the Han Dynasty (202 BC—220 AD). Records of the Chung Dynasty (960—1279 AD) show a game similar to Mah Jong, known as Ma Chuek, which was played with forty curved pieces similar to dominoes. Essentially a gambling game, Mah Jong as we know it developed in the late eighteen hundreds, probably originating in the Ningpo region. It was further developed in various parts of China, each region forming its own rules with special hands. Because the Chinese learned the game by watching play during childhood, there were no written instructions, nor recognised standardised rules.

Sets of tiles were found in various parts of the world around the turn of the century. It was known that they were part of a game, but the method of play was unknown.

Joseph P. Babcock, who lived in Soochow (now Suzhou) and worked there as a representative of the Standard Oil Company, was the first to painstakingly collect and interpret the many conflicting variations throughout China. Arabic numbers engraved on the tiles were first introduced by Mr Babcock in 1920, when he imported to the USA sets of tiles in sufficient quantity. He simplified the game and introduced a standard set of rules which could be easily understood, giving us the game of Mah Jong as we know it today.

Mah Jong is a game for two, three, four or five people, although it is usually played by four people playing as individuals, not as partners. The first description of the game will refer to one played by four people, the Western version of the game commonly played in Australia.

In turn players draw one tile at a time from a stack—known as the wall—or pick up a discard, then put out one tile.

The Objective

The objective of the game is to obtain a complete set of four defined groups of three or four tiles and one pair.

In the *Chinese version* of the game, suit tiles in any one group must be from one suit, but the hand may contain groups of differing suits, or Honours.

In the *Western version*, the suit tiles in an ordinary winning hand are all of one suit, referred to as a 'cleared suit'. The hand may include Honour tiles. Special hands, designed to broaden the scope of the game, were also added.

The first player to achieve this structure, although not necessarily obtaining the highest score, wins the hand. The winner does not have to pay any other player.

The player with the highest score after a predetermined number of hands has been played wins the game.

A TYPICAL CHINESE HAND (ANY SUITS AND MAY CONTAIN ANY NUMBER OF CHOWS)

**THE OBJECTIVE OF THE GAME IS TO OBTAIN A COMPLETE SET OF FOUR
DEFINED GROUPS OF THREE OR FOUR TILES AND ONE PAIR.**

A TYPICAL WESTERN HAND (ANY ONE SUIT AND MAY CONTAIN ONLY ONE CHOW)

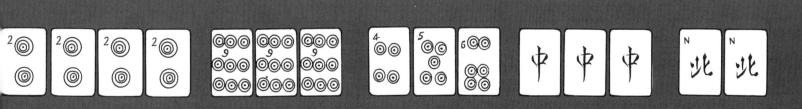

See ordinary hand, p.34

SEAT SELECTION

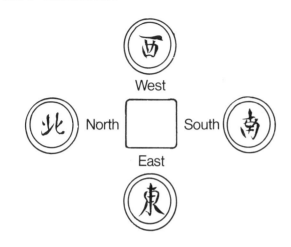

West

North   South

East

THE GREAT WALL OF CHINA

West

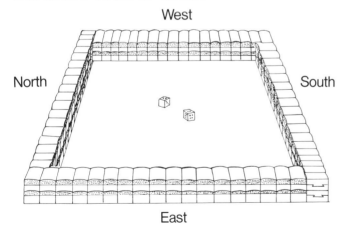

North   South

East

Let's Play

Rules

1. Seat selection and lead   The four players in turn throw two dice. The highest total leads the game and becomes East Wind.

East Wind selects a seat.
West Wind sits opposite East.
South Wind sits to *right* of East.
North Wind sits opposite South.

Note that this does not follow the normal geographical relationships between the compass points.

2. The wind discs and the racks   Wind discs may be used for seat selection (see page 10) and to indicate the Wind of the Round. If one rack is red it is passed to the player who is East Wind.

3. Shuffling the tiles   144 tiles (or 136 if you are playing without Flowers or Seasons) are placed face down on the table and shuffled. This is sometimes known as the 'Twittering of the Sparrows'.

4. Building the wall   Assuming all the tiles are in play, each player takes 18 tiles at random and arranges them in front of him, long sides touching, then places another 18 tiles on top, thus forming a *wall*. The four walls should be joined at the corners—they represent the Great Wall of China.

5. Selection of wall to be broken   Two dice are now thrown by East to determine:

(a) Which wall is to be broken, and
(b) Where the break will occur.

With the sum of the two dice, East counts in an anticlockwise

BREAKING THE WALL (PLAN)

West 3,7,11

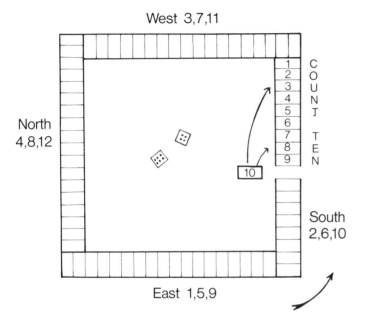

North
4,8,12

South
2,6,10

East 1,5,9

DETAIL OF SOUTH WALL

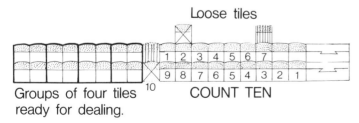

Groups of four tiles
ready for dealing.

Loose tiles

COUNT TEN

East receives first group of tiles, then South, etc.

direction, starting with his own wall as number 1, until he reaches the number thrown. The following table will save you counting.

Number Thrown	Player to Break Wall
5 or 9	East Wind
2, 6 or 10	South Wind
3, 7 or 11	West Wind
4, 8 or 12	North Wind

East Wind picks up the dice and places them on his rack.

6. Breaking the wall When the wall to be opened has been determined, the player who built that wall counts the tiles from the right-hand side until the same number thrown on the dice is reached—these two tiles are removed and placed face downwards on top of the second and seventh tiles on the right side of the break. They are now known as the *loose* tiles.

7. Loose tiles Loose tiles are used to replace tiles taken for Kongs, Flowers and Seasons during the course of play. When each two are used, starting with the tile further from the break, two more tiles are taken from the end of the wall to the right of the break, and positioned on top of the wall as replacements.

8. Dealing Beginning with East, each player draws two pairs (four tiles) from the left side of the opening, placing them on his rack. Thus East draws first, followed by South, West, then North (proceeding in an anticlockwise direction), until each player has taken 12 tiles. East Wind then takes the next tile from the top row, the remaining three players each taking one tile in turn. East Wind then takes one more tile, making 14 tiles, while the other players each have 13 tiles. East then makes the first discard. It is helpful if each player announces the number of tiles taken after each turn.

9. Tile arrangement The tiles are placed on a rack or on the table with the faces obscured from other players, and sorted into suits. It helps to place the Honours at one end and push all the tiles together, thus not revealing the number of sets held. Change the arrangement from time to time to keep the opponents guessing!

10. Flowers and Seasons   There are four Flower tiles and four Season tiles, making eight in all. These tiles play no part in the game. They are bonus tiles, introducing the element of luck and adding extra value to the hand. Season and Flower tiles dealt to a player are placed face up on top of the rack and a loose tile taken from the wall as a replacement. Should two or more players be dealt one or more of these tiles, East takes the replacements first, followed by South, West and North in turn. Season and Flower tiles may only be drawn from the wall, and are not discarded. When drawn during play they are exposed face up on top of the rack and a loose tile taken immediately as a replacement to correct the number in the hand.

11. Play   To start the play, East Wind discards one of his 14 tiles, laying it in the centre of the table face up. Each discard should be named clearly as a courtesy to the other players. If no other player requires this tile, South has the next turn of play and draws the next tile from the wall, the order of play being East, South, West, North ('Eat Soy With Noodles').

12. A complete turn   A player's turn may commence when he takes a turn in the normal progression of play, drawing a tile from the open end of the wall or picking up the last discard for an exposed Chow. *Any* player, whether it is his normal turn or not, may call 'Pung', 'Kong' or 'Mah Jong' and obtain a tile just discarded. His turn is completed when he has discarded a tile, face up in the centre of the table. No player may draw from the wall until the discard of the previous player has been made.

13. Turns lost   When a player pungs or kongs a discard the player to his right takes the next turn unless there is another call of 'Pung' or 'Mah Jong'. The players between the discarder and the caller lose their turn.

14. The discard   Each player tries gradually to improve his hand while thoughtfully discarding the tile least likely to enable an opponent to win. Watch discards carefully because the discards of other players do indicate their intentions to a certain extent. A claimed discard must remain visible to the other players.

15. To Pung   Any player who has two identical tiles in his hand may call 'Pung' immediately a third matching tile is discarded, claiming it and placing in *on top* of his rack with the other two tiles from his hand to form an *exposed Pung*. He then discards a tile. The fourth identical tile may not be added to form a Kong unless that player draws it from the wall himself.

16. Exposed Kong   Should a player be holding three identical tiles when the fourth is discarded, he may call 'Kong' and must then expose all four tiles on top of the rack—this is known as an *exposed Kong*. A player *must take an extra tile* from the loose tiles and place it in his concealed hand when any Kong is made, otherwise he will not have enough tiles to go Mah Jong.

The player may, however, pung the discard and lay down three tiles while keeping the fourth concealed, preferring to hold it for a possible Chow. He has the option of adding this tile to his Pung to form a Kong in any one of his subsequent turns.

17. Concealed Kong   Before drawing the replacement loose tile for a concealed Kong, the four tiles of the Kong must be placed on the top of the rack with the two middle tiles turned face down. Some clubs allow the Kong to be entirely concealed, but this must be established before play commences.

18. Robbing the Kong   Should a player with an exposed Pung draw the fourth matching tile from the wall he may join it to his Pung to form a Kong. If he does so, however, any other player who can use this tile immediately to go Mah Jong may claim it.

19. Chow from discard   If no player pungs a discard, the player on the right of the discarder may claim this tile to complete a Chow if he holds the other two tiles. The three tiles must then be exposed on top of the rack. Another player may claim this tile for a Chow only if the tile completes his hand to go Mah Jong.

20. Tile precedence Should the same discard be needed for a Chow by a player on the right of the discarder and for a Pung or Kong by another player, the Pung or Kong has precedence, but a player requiring that tile to go Mah Jong takes precedence over all others. If two players require the same tile to win, the player next in turn claims the tile.

21. Dead tiles Once a tile has been discarded and not claimed immediately by another player it is known as a *dead tile* and plays no further part in the game.

22. Fishing or calling When a player requires only one more tile to complete his hand for Mah Jong, his hand is said to be 'fishing' or 'calling'. When a player is fishing for a special hand, and another player goes Mah Jong, certain conditions apply to the scoring (see page 32).

23. Game! Each player in turn to the right continues to draw and discard until one player announces 'Mah Jong!' or the hand is drawn. The player to win must show all his tiles face upwards. The concealed tiles are displayed as shown in the scoring diagrams.

24. Settlement The player to win counts his score and is the first to be paid. All players pay the winner, who does not pay anyone. When the winner has been paid, all the other players expose their hands, total their scores and settle the differences by exchanging counters.

East Wind pays and receives double. If he loses, he pays the other players double their scores and if he wins, he receives double his score.

25. Changing winds Should East Wind go Mah Jong he remains East Wind until another player goes Mah Jong.

Should East Wind not go Mah Jong (but another player does), the title of East Wind passes on to the *next player in an anti-clockwise direction*, regardless of who went Mah Jong. Each player then becomes a different wind, i.e. South becomes the new East Wind, West becomes South, North becomes West, and East becomes North.

26. Drawn hand Should no player complete a hand for Mah Jong before all tiles have been drawn from the wall, all hands are abandoned and no-one scores. Tiles are turned face down and shuffled, the wall rebuilt and a Goulash is played.

27. The Goulash This takes place when a game is drawn (no player goes Mah Jong). The preliminaries for a Goulash are exactly the same as those for a standard game. After examining the tiles dealt, however, three tiles are exchanged with the player opposite. Then East exchanges three tiles with South, West exchanges with North. Lastly East exchanges three tiles with North while West and South exchange. Thus the tiles are exchanged three times. East Wind remains East Wind for the Goulash but then loses the privilege, regardless of who wins.

No Chows are permitted in a Goulash hand unless part of a specialty hand (see illustrations), therefore no doubles are awarded for no Chows. (See g., page 25.)

(a) The four *blank tiles* may be inserted and used as joker tiles. In this case the walls opposite East and West will contain 38 tiles instead of 36, *or*

(b) the four tiles of the 2 Bamboos may be used as jokers.

A player may nominate wild tiles or jokers as any tile. Should an exposed Kong include a joker, and the player draw the fourth matching tile, he may remove the joker and use it again.

Pool If agreed prior to playing the Goulash, each player may place a 200 point counter, or any predetermined sum, into a 'kitty' which the winner takes.

If there is another draw, a Goulash is played again, East Wind remains East and each player puts another counter into the pool.

Courtesies

1. The player whose wall is being used swings the open end towards the centre of the table within easy reach of all players.

2. Lose no time in drawing and discarding, for a slow player tends to spoil the game for others. Instinct is often best when discarding, especially in the early stages of the game.

3. Avoid comments on tiles drawn or tiles held.

4. When considering which tile to discard, do so while the other players are taking their turns. It is a good idea to keep the tiles to be discarded to one side, enabling you to discard quickly.

5. When a player, in his turn, has drawn the next tile from the wall and placed it on his rack, it is too late for another player to pung the previous discard.

Reshuffle A player may request a reshuffle if he is dealt no Winds, Dragons, Pairs, Pung or Chow, Terminals, Seasons or Flowers. The other players are obliged to abandon their hands.

Penalties

1. Too many tiles A player holding too many tiles may not correct the number. He is not permitted to go Mah Jong, and scores nothing.

2. Too few tiles Any player holding too few tiles may not correct the error after discarding. He may score his hand, but is unable to go Mah Jong.

3. Declaration of a false Mah Jong Play may continue if the other players have not exposed their hands, but if they have, the player making this mistake must pay a half-limit to each of the other players.

4. Discarded tiles May not be reclaimed.

5. Careless discards If a player has a sufficient number of exposed tiles to indicate the tile needed to complete his hand and another player discards that tile, the player responsible for that discard must pay not only his debt to the winner, but also those of the other two losers.

This rule does not apply if the player discarding the winning tile was also Fishing or holding at least three doubles.

Strategies

1. Count the tiles at the beginning and during the game to ensure that you have the correct number.

2. Consider carefully before taking a discarded tile to form a Chow, especially in the early stages of the game.

3. A Wind or Dragon tile should not be discarded in the latter stages of the game unless it forms the fourth tile of an exposed Pung. Discarding these tiles in the early stages of the game gives the other players less opportunity to form Pungs.

4. Do not adhere to one arrangement of tiles held, but vary their positions. Keep as much as possible concealed.

5. Discard thoughtfully, especially in the latter stages of the game. Note tiles which may be discarded with safety.

6. Watch exposed and discarded tiles, as they may indicate a change of plan.

7. If possible, try to go Mah Jong in more than one way, especially in the Chinese game.

8. A Kong should not be made in haste. If you hold a concealed Pung of a suit tile and the fourth is discarded, it may be claimed as a Pung and joined with two of the tiles, leaving one tile in hand to form a possible Chow. This fourth tile may be joined to the exposed Pung to form an exposed Kong during a subsequent turn.

A Hand

A hand begins when the tiles have been dealt and ends when one player completes the necessary groups with his tiles for Mah Jong or the hand is drawn.

A Round

A round is finished when each player has completed a turn as East Wind. It therefore consists of a minimum of four hands (with four players); however, should East Wind win, he remains East Wind, resulting in an extra hand for each time he wins or the hand is drawn.

A Game

A game ends at an agreed time or when East, South, West and North have all been the Wind of the Round.

The Wind of the Round (or Prevailing Wind)

During the first round, the prevailing wind is East.
During the second round, the prevailing wind is South.
During the third round, the prevailing wind is West.
During the fourth round, the prevailing wind is North.

Extra points are awarded for holding tiles of one's own wind or the wind of the round or both.

Counters (Western Game)

No. of Counters	Points per Counter	Total Points
10	100	1000
8	500	4000
7	1000	7000
1	4000	4000
	TOTAL	16000

Although counters may vary in value from set to set, each player needs to start with the same number of points.

Generally the pay is made to the nearest 100 points—over 50 counts as 100, 50 or less counts to the 100 below.

Scoring

When a player completes a winning combination all the tiles are placed face up.

Exposed tiles are those which have been taken from discards and have been placed face up on the top of the rack or the table.

Concealed tiles are those concealed when all the tiles on the rack have been drawn from the wall.

The basic scoring combinations are Pungs and Kongs. Concealed Pungs are shown with the centre tile turned face down. Concealed Kongs are shown with the two centre tiles turned face down (see illustration, page 17).

The limit As it is possible to score over 63 000 points in one hand, at the start of a game a limit should be arranged.

Examples of commonly used limits:

Chinese, not using Seasons	300points
Chinese, using Seasons	500
Western, using Seasons	1000
Modern American, using Seasons	500

Levels of settlement

Beginners Score and pay winning hand only.
Intermediate Score and pay winning and fishing hands.
Advanced Score and pay all hands.

The Ground Score

ALL PLAYERS		POINTS AWARDED	
		Exposed	*Concealed*
PUNGS	Suit tiles 2 to 8	2	4
	Winds, Dragons, 1s and 9s	4	8
KONGS	Suit tiles 2 to 8	8	16
	Winds, Dragons, 1s and 9s	16	32
CHOWS		0	0
FLOWERS and SEASONS (if used)		4 for each	

(a) Any pair of Dragons	2
(b) A pair of player's own Wind	2
(c) A pair of Wind of the Round	2
(d) Claiming first discard made by East Wind	2

Winning hand only—In addition to the above:

(e) For going Mah Jong by making a Chow with a tile in the only possible places (see illustration page 25)	2
(f) For drawing the winning tile from the wall	2
(g) For completing the Pair with the winning tile	2
(h) For going Mah Jong	20

These scores are known as the *ground* or *basic* score and are added before the score is doubled for any Honour combinations.

THE ONLY POSSIBLE PLACES TO COMPLETE A HAND FOR A WIN:

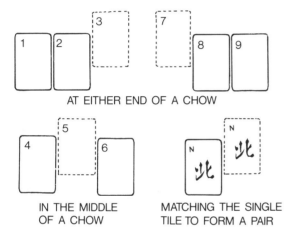

AT EITHER END OF A CHOW

IN THE MIDDLE
OF A CHOW

MATCHING THE SINGLE
TILE TO FORM A PAIR

Doubling the Ground Score

All players—one double for:

(a) Each Pung or Kong of Dragons
(b) Pung or Kong of the player's own Wind
(c) Pung or Kong of the Wind of the Round
(d) Holding the player's own Season
(e) Holding the player's own Flower

Winning and Fishing Hands only—one double, in addition to the above, for:
(f) Any one suit with Winds or Dragons or both
(g) No Chows
(h) Going Mah Jong   (i)   With a loose tile off the Wall,
                       (ii) With the last remaining tile of the Wall,
                       (iii) By robbing the Kong

Two doubles

(i) A concealed Mah Jong—all tiles drawn from the Wall.

All players—three doubles for:

(j) All one suit—no Winds, no Dragons. If this hand contains the player's own Season, own Flower, and no Chows, add one double for each.
(k) Honour tiles only (this includes one double for all Pungs). Add one double for each a, b, c, d, e (as above) and cleared suit if the terminals are of the same suit.
Bouquet of Seasons (this includes one double for own Season).
Bouquet of Flowers (this includes one double for own Flower).

Please see the example of scoring on the next page.

25

For example, let us suppose that West goes Mah Jong with an ordinary, one suit hand. The Wind of the Round is East. Ground score is totalled first.

1 Pung of exposed West Winds	= 4	points
1 Pung of concealed 3 Bamboos	= 4	
1 Kong of exposed Green Dragons	= 16	
1 Kong of concealed 1 Bamboos	= 32	
1 Pair of East Wind (Wind of the Round)	= 2	
which was drawn from the wall	= 2	
Flower number 3 (own Flower)	= 4	
For going Mah Jong	= 20	
Total ground score =	84	points

Doubles are then totalled.

Mah Jong with one suit with Winds and Dragons	= 1	double
No Chows	= 1	
Kong of Green Dragons	= 1	
Pung of own Wind	= 1	
Own Flower	= 1	
Total number of doubles	= 5	

Take discarded tiles from the centre to indicate the ground score numerically. Use tiles placed on their sides to indicate the number of doubles, as in the illustration.

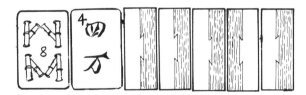

West Wind doubles his ground score of 84 five times (refer to the doubling table). The score is 2688. This score is a limit.

South and North Winds pay 1000 points to West Wind, while East Wind must pay 2000 points to West Wind.

Versions of the Game

The Chinese (and original) version is easy to learn, appears simple but should not be underestimated, for the more it is played, the more the mystery and subtlety of the game reveals itself.

The Western way offers variety of a different kind. The illustrations from pages 32 to 58 will assist in the construction of Special hands.

Finally there is the modern American version, more complex in structure but with a great range of variations and a most acceptable scoring system; it is an extension of both the Chinese and Western games. For details of this version see *Mah Jong, Anyone? A Manual of Modern Play* by Kitty Strauser and Lucille Evans, published by Tuttle.

The Chinese Game

Newcomers to Mah Jong will find the Chinese game an excellent starting point.

This is a fast moving, exciting game requiring quick thinking and a mind capable of constantly adapting to the tile changes which occur throughout the game. The Chinese learn Mah Jong as children—to them it is almost a way of life. They prefer to play without the Flower and Season tiles for an ideal combination of skill and chance.

Mah Jong is easier to learn than chess and provokes less controversy than some card games as no partnerships are formed. The game appeals to many differing temperaments. Interest is sustained, for even a poor hand has countless possibilities; it is a game rich in variety. Play follows the same procedure as in the Western game, with the exception of the Flower and Season tiles. Special hands are not generally played but there are exceptions—see page 30.

Play, therefore, is with 136 tiles—two rows of 17 tiles to each wall. The last 14 tiles are known as the Dead Part of the Wall and are not used. A small division is sometimes made between the two sections. If a Kong is formed during the game, however, a loose tile is taken from this portion of the Wall. (See diagram, page 19.)

Beginners should set up the tiles and practice setting up different hands and scoring so that they become familiar with the tiles. (*Scoring*, see page 24.)

The Objective

The objective of the Chinese game is to be the first player to complete a winning combination consisting of *four* groups of Pungs (or Kongs) and Chows, plus one pair. The suits may be mixed and may include Winds or Dragons or both (see illustration page 29). Any number of Chows are permitted. Fourteen tiles are required to go Mah Jong, the last tile being taken into the hand and no discard made.

The game really offers a choice—either to go Mah Jong with a low score or to aim for a higher score with a better tile combination. The risk is that another player may go Mah Jong with a low score. The aim, however, is to be the first player to go Mah Jong, whatever the score may be. Try to leave as many openings as possible to complete the hand. *Woo* means 'I win' and is the term used for Mah Jong. The scores in the Chinese game tend to be lower, and the values of the counters vary accordingly.

The counters

	Points	Total
10 counters (with two black dots)	2	20
8 counters (with ten black dots)	10	80
9 counters (with one red dot)	100	900
2 counters (with five red dots)	500	1000

Total	29 counters to each player and a total of 2000 points

A limit is set, usually 300 points with no Seasons or Flowers, or 500 points where Seasons and Flowers are included.

Drawn game If no player calls 'Woo' before the last 14 tiles have been used, no scores are counted, the tiles are shuffled, the wall rebuilt and another hand is played. East Wind remains East and continues as East if he wins. Each player puts a predetermined amount into the kitty which the winner takes as an added bonus. The Chinese do not play Goulash.

Scoring a Chinese Hand

Scoring is as described on pages 24 and 25, with the following addition:

   A non-scoring hand (4 chows and a worthless pair) is awarded 10 points.

Beginners are advised to score only the hand to go Mah Jong. More experienced players should score all hands—it is not always the hand that goes Mah Jong which scores the most points.

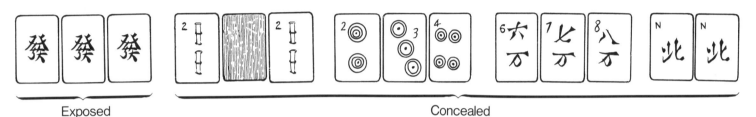

Exposed | Concealed

1. First add the winner's points for the scoring groups (page 24).
2. Add any extra points including 20 points for winning.
3. Add these sums together to obtain the ground score.
4. Count the number of doubles which apply. (Use the doubling table on the inside back cover.)
Settlement   See page 21.

Example of a completed hand held by North Wind.

Counting the points

Pung of Green Dragons (exposed)	4 points
Pung of 2 Bamboos (concealed)	4 points
Chow of Circle suit	0 points
Chow of Character suit	0 points
Pair of North Winds	2 points
Score for winning the hand	20 points
	30 points

Count one double for a Pung of Dragons   =   60 points

   Therefore South and West pay 60 points to North, while East pays 120 points to North.

   The losers may choose to balance their losses between them.

Special hands are not generally played but the following hands may be included if agreed (numbers refer to illustrations):

3. *Heavenly Twins*
5. *Gates of Heaven (Nine Gates)*
12. *Unique Wonder (Thirteen Orphans)*
15. *Heads and Tails* (all terminals)
25. *Imperial Jade* (all green)
33. *All Winds and Dragons*
34. *Three Great Scholars* (Pungs of all Dragons)
35. *The Four Blessings* (The Four Wind hand)

A few other Special hands do occur, but only rarely.

All Kong: Four Kongs and one Pair, all in one suit. Either Winds, Dragons or both may be included. **Score: Limit**

Mixed Pung: Four Pungs and a Pair in any of the three suits. Either Winds, Dragons or both may be included. Every tile including the last must be drawn from the wall. *Score:* Limit

Heavenly Paradise: Pung or Kong of green, red and white Dragons plus a Pair of any Wind, Pung or Kong of own Wind, when it is Wind of the Round. A Bouquet must also be held. **Score: every counter on table**

Heaven's Grace: When East Wind finds his hand complete with his original 14 tiles. **Score: Double limit**

Earth's Grace: When any player finds he is one tile short of Mah Jong and goes Mah Jong with East's first discard. **Score: Limit**

Plucking the Plum Blossom from the Roof: The player must be calling for 5 Circles, and takes a loose tile which is the 5 Circles. **Score: Limit**

Picking the Moon from the Bottom of the Sea: The player is fishing for 1 Circles and takes the last tile on the wall which is 1 Circles. **Score: Limit**

Mah Jong Terms

A summary designed for those players with some knowledge of the game.

Suits Bamboo, Circle and Character.

Winds East, South, West and North.

Dragons Green, Red and White.

Pung A group of three identical tiles.

Kong A group of four identical tiles.

Chow A run of three consecutive tiles *only* in the same suit, e.g. 4,5,6 of Bamboo.

Pair A pair of identical tiles, also known as the 'Sparrow's Head', the 'Eyes' or a 'Pillow'.

Basic Mah Jong Hand—Western Consists of four Pungs or Kongs and a Pair (may substitute one Chow for a pung), all in the same suit. May include Honours.

Basic Mah Jong Hand—Chinese As above, but the suits may be mixed and any number of Chows are permitted.

Terminals 1s and 9s of each suit.

Honour Tiles Winds, Dragons and terminals.

Loose Tiles Tiles to replace Kongs, Seasons and Flowers.

Dead Tiles Tiles unclaimed when discarded may not be claimed later in the game.

Fishing or Calling When a player is waiting for one tile to complete his hand.

Goulash Exchange of tiles before play when no player in the previous game went Mah Jong.

Flowers,	1. Spring	Plum	East
Seasons	2. Summer	Orchid	South
and Winds	3. Autumn	Chrysanthemum	West
	4. Winter	Bamboo	North

Bouquet Complete set of 4 Season or Flower tiles 1–4 all in the same colour.

Teaching Children

Mah Jong may be understood and played by young children with the assistance of a parent or grandparent (who may have a little more time to spare).

Children like to get on with the game, so abandon (temporarily) the protocol.

1. Remove the Seasons and Flowers.
2. Spread all 136 tiles face down on the table.
3. Two dice are rolled by each player to establish who is East. For seating see illustration, page 18.
4. Each player takes four tiles in the order East, South, West and North. Dealing continues in this way until all four players have twelve tiles each.
5. Each player then takes one tile and East takes a final extra tile so that East has 14 tiles and the other players have 13 tiles each.

This is the original form of the game, used before unscrupulous players rendered the building of the walls a necessity to guard against dishonest play.

Now follow instruction 11, Play, on page 20, making the objective that of the Chinese game. See pages 28 and 29.

This game will capture the child's attention because it is not only easier to understand but also faster to play. Once the main objective of the game is grasped, the construction of the walls should be introduced along with the scoring.

How to Use the Illustrations

The following Special hands have been arranged in groups to assist the player to find alternative hands with ease. The progression from one hand to the next will be of great assistance to the beginner who often finds confusing the necessary change from one hand to another.

The logical progression is well illustrated on page 39. Supposing you start to collect the Honour tiles for a Unique Wonder but another player produces a Kong of an Honour tile. You convert the hand to an All Pair Honour hand, but as the game proceeds, collect a Pung or two of Honour tiles. Your hand may then be changed to an All Honour hand.

Mah Jong terms and the synopsis of Special hands will help those beyond the beginner stage.

Further variations (see page 51) have been included for players needing a refreshing change. They may be added to the Special hands a few at a time.

'Concealed **tiles**' (except last tile) means the last tile may be taken from either the wall or a discard.

'Exposed **tiles**' means a Pung may be made from a discard.

Beginners should become familiar with scoring by playing the ordinary Mah Jong hand before attempting any special hands.

Scoring for Special Hands

Special hands were introduced into the game at the turn of the century. In these hands the tiles form a pre-arranged combination. The groups of tiles do not score as in an ordinary suit hand, the score being determined by the ease or difficulty of obtaining the combinations. A **limit** of 1000 points is set. The player achieving a Special hand will score either a half-limit, limit or double-limit, according to the score allotted for that particular hand.

Scoring for a Fishing Hand   When a player needs only one tile to complete his hand he is said to be 'fishing'—he should announce this. If he is fishing for a Special hand the score will be varied as follows when the limit is 1000 points:

Half-limit hand scores one-fifth of the limit   = 200 points
Limit hand scores two-fifths of the limit   = 400 points
Double limit hand scores one-half of the limit = 500 points
As with other scores, East Wind pays or receives double.

Special hands tend to speed up the scoring, for the only hands for which the Ground score and number of doubles need to be calculated are the Ordinary cleared suit, Purity, All Honour and Concealed Mah Jong (Buried Treasure) hands. For these hands all players score as described on page 24. When fishing for these hands, score in the same way, without the bonus of 20 points for going Mah Jong.

Bouquet   If a player draws a Bouquet (a set of four Season or Flower tiles) while attempting a Special hand, each of the other players immediately gives this player one 1000-point counter and the four tiles are turned face down.

Special Hands

Score: See score-sheet, pp.24 and 25

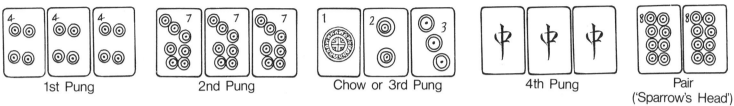

| 1st Pung | 2nd Pung | Chow or 3rd Pung | 4th Pung | Pair ('Sparrow's Head') |

Any one suit

Pungs and Kongs and a Pair. A Chow may be substituted for a Pung.

May include Winds, Dragons or both.

If all tiles including the last are drawn from the wall the hand is known as a concealed Mah Jong and scores 2 extra doubles.

---

2. PURITY HAND

Score: THREE DOUBLES PLUS EXTRAS (see score-sheet)

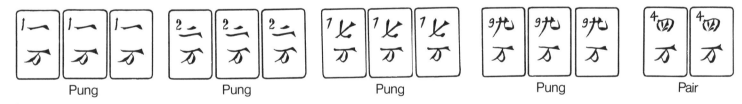

| Pung | Pung | Pung | Pung | Pair |

Any one suit.

Pungs or Kongs and a Pair.   No Winds or Dragons.

A Chow may be substituted for a Pung.

If all tiles including the last are drawn from the wall the hand is known as a concealed Mah Jong and scores 2 extra doubles.

3. HEAVENLY TWINS

Score: LIMIT

  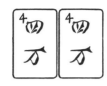

Any one suit.
7 Pairs.

No Winds or Dragons.
Concealed (except last tile).

---

4. ALL PAIR

Score: HALF LIMIT

 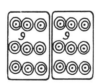

Any one suit.
7 Pairs.
With Winds, Dragons or both.

Concealed (except last tile).

5. GATES OF HEAVEN

Score: LIMIT

 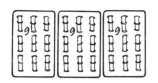 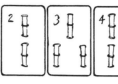 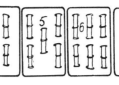

any tile 2–8 paired

Any one suit.
Pung of 1s. Pung of 9s
Run of 2–8. Any tile 2–8 paired

No Winds or Dragons.
Concealed (except last tile).

---

6. RUN, PUNG AND A PAIR

Score: LIMIT

         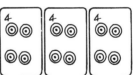

Any one suit.
Run of 1–9.
A Pung and a Pair.

No Winds or Dragons.
Concealed (except last tile).

7. GERTIE'S GARTER

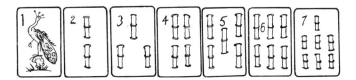 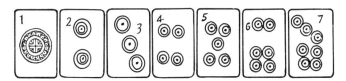

Run of 1–7 in one suit.
Run of 1–7 in another suit.

No Winds or Dragons.
Concealed (except last tile).

8. KNITTING

Score: HALF LIMIT

 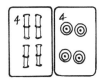 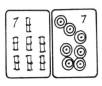

Two suits.
One tile from one suit paired with corresponding number from the other suit.

No Winds or Dragons.
Concealed (except last tile).

9. TRIPLE KNITTING

Score: HALF LIMIT

 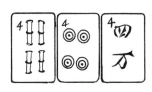 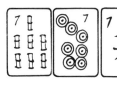 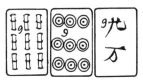 

4 Sets and a knitting Pair.
One of each suit of same number.

No Winds or Dragons.
Concealed (except last tile).

10. WRIGGLY SNAKE

Score: LIMIT

Any one suit.
Run of 1–9. One of each Wind
Any tile paired

No Dragons.
Concealed (except last tile).

---

11. CONCEALED MAH JONG (BURIED TREASURE)

Score: 10 POINTS FOR NON-SCORING HAND

Any one suit.
As many Chows or Pungs as desired. May include Winds, Dragons or both and a Pair.
Every tile from wall including last.
If all the tiles are in same suit (as in above example) score 3 doubles (as for Purity).

No Kongs.
Score 2 doubles plus extras.

12. UNIQUE WONDER

Score: DOUBLE LIMIT

 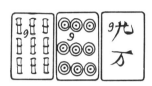  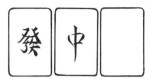 Any tile paired

1s and 9s from each suit.
One of each Wind.
One of each Dragon. Any tile paired.

Concealed (except last tile).

---

13. ALL PAIR HONOURS

Score: LIMIT

 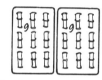 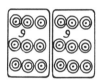 

Pairs of 1s and 9s in any suit.
May include Winds, Dragons or both.
May be Winds and Dragons only, or 1s and 9s only.

Concealed (except last tile)

---

14. ALL HONOUR HAND

Score: THREE DOUBLES PLUS EXTRAS (see score-sheet)

 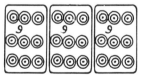   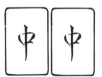

Pungs or Kongs of 1s and 9s in any suit with Winds, Dragons or both.
A Pair of Honours.

Exposed.

If all tiles including last are drawn from the wall the hand is known as a concealed Mah Jong and scores 2 extra doubles.

15. HEADS AND TAILS (1s AND 9s)

Score: LIMIT

 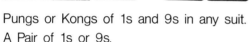 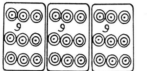 

Pungs or Kongs of 1s and 9s in any suit.
A Pair of 1s or 9s.

No Winds or Dragons.
Exposed.

---

16. CHINESE ODDS

Score: LIMIT

Any one suit.
Pungs or Kongs of odd numbers.
Any Pair of odd numbers.

No Winds or Dragons.
Exposed.

17. DRAGONFLY

Score: LIMIT (if all tiles from wall except last)
HALF LIMIT (Pungs from discard)

 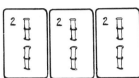 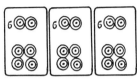  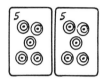

One of each Dragon.
Pung or Kong in each of the three suits.
A Pair of any suit.

No Winds.

---

18. WINDY CHOW

Score: HALF LIMIT

 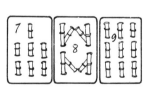 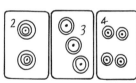 

One of each Wind with one paired.
A Chow in each suit.

No Dragons.
Concealed (except last tile).

19. WINDY ONES

Score: LIMIT (if all Pungs concealed)
HALF LIMIT (Pungs from discard)

One of each Wind.

Any Wind paired.

Pungs or Kongs of each of the 1s in each suit.

No Dragons.

---

20. WINDY NINES

Score: LIMIT (if all pungs concealed)
HALF LIMIT (Pungs from discard)

 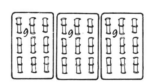 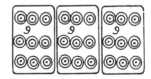 

One of each Wind.

Any Wind paired.

Pungs or Kongs of each of the 9s in each suit.

No Dragons.

21. GRETA'S GARDEN

Score: LIMIT

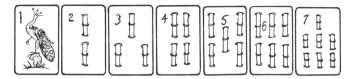 

Any one suit.
Run of 1–7.
One of each Wind. One of each Dragon.

No Pairs.
Concealed (except last tile).

---

22. GRETA'S DRAGON

Score: LIMIT

Any one suit.
Run of 1–7.
One of each Wind. Pung of any Dragons.

No Pairs.
Concealed (except last tile).

23. SPARROW'S SANCTUARY

Score: LIMIT

   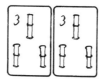 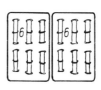 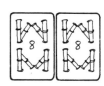

2 Pairs of 1 Bamboos ('Sparrow's Head').

1 Pair of each green Bamboos (2,3,4,6 and 8).

No Winds or Dragons.

Concealed (except last tile)

---

24. ALL PAIR JADE

Score: LIMIT

 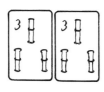 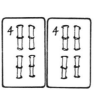 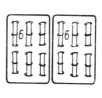 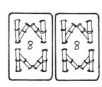

6 Pairs of green Bamboos (2,3,4,6 and 8).

(2 Pairs do not count as a Kong)

At least one Pair of Green Dragons.

No Winds.

Concealed (except last tile).

25. IMPERIAL JADE

Score: DOUBLE LIMIT

 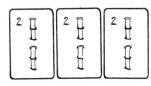 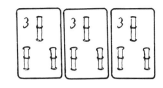 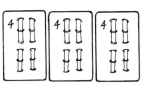 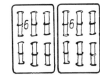

Pung of Green Dragons.

Pungs or Kongs of Green Bamboos (2,3,4,6 and 8).

Pair of Green Bamboos.

No Winds.

Exposed.

One Chow allowed (beware of making Kongs—the fourth tile may be required to form a Chow).

26. LILY OF THE VALLEY

Score: DOUBLE LIMIT

 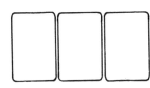 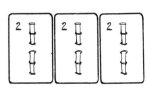 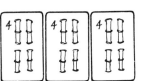 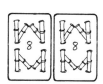

Pung or Kong of Green Dragons.

Pung or Kong of White Dragons.

2 Pungs or Kongs of Green Bamboos. Pair of Green Bamboos (2,3,4,6 and 8).

No Winds.

Exposed.

27. ALL PAIR RUBY JADE

Score: LIMIT

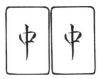 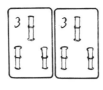 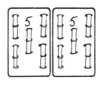   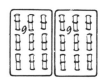

Pair of Red Dragons.
Pair of Green Dragons.
5 Pairs of Red and Green Bamboos, mixed.

No Winds.
Concealed (except last tile).

---

28. RUBY JADE

Score: LIMIT

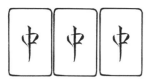   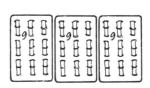 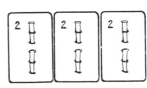

Pung of Red Dragons. Pung of Green Dragons.
Pung of Red Bamboos. Pung of Green Bamboos.
Pair of any Bamboos.

No Winds.
Exposed.

29. ROYAL RUBY

Score: DOUBLE LIMIT

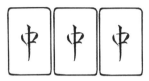   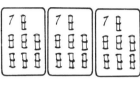 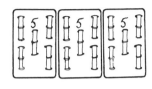 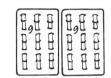

Pungs or Kongs of Red Dragons and Red Bamboos (1,5,7 and 9).
Pair of Red Bamboos.

No Winds.
No Chows.
Exposed.

30. RED LILY

Score: DOUBLE LIMIT

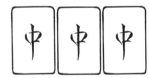 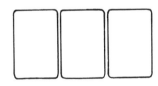 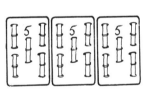 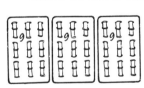 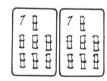

Pung or Kong of Red Dragons. Pung or Kong of White Dragons.
2 Pungs or Kongs of Red Bamboos. Pair of Red Bamboos (1,5,7 and 9).

No Winds.
Exposed.

31. RED LANTERN

Score: DOUBLE LIMIT (if all tiles from wall except last)
LIMIT (Pungs from discard)

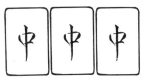 

| Any tile 1–7 paired |

Pung or Kong of Red Dragons.

Pung or Kong of Own Wind.

Run of 1–7 in same suit. Any tile 1–7 paired.

---

32. WINDY DRAGONS

Score: LIMIT

      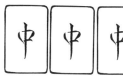

Pair of each Wind.

2 Pungs of any Dragons.

Dragons may be punged from a discard.

---

33. ALL WINDS AND DRAGONS

Score: LIMIT

 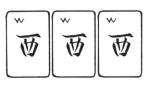    

Pungs or Kongs of Winds and Dragons only.

Pair of Winds or Dragons.

Exposed.

34. THREE GREAT SCHOLARS (DRAGONS)

Score: LIMIT

Pungs or Kongs of all three Dragons.
Pung, Kong or a Chow and a Pair of any one suit or Winds.

Exposed.
A limit is scored for any hand
containing the Three Great Scholars.

---

35. THE FOUR BLESSINGS (WINDS)

Score: LIMIT

 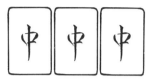 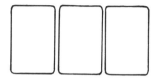

Pungs or Kongs of each of the four Winds and a Pair of anything.

Exposed.
A limit is scored for any hand
containing Pungs of each Wind.

Summary of Scoring for Special Hands

(numbers relate to illustrations)

Half-Limit

4. All Pair
8. Knitting
9. Triple Knitting
17. Dragonfly (Pungs from a discard)
18. Windy Chow
19. Windy Ones (Pungs from a discard)
20. Windy Nines (Pungs from a discard)
47. Five Odd Honours

Limit

3. Heavenly Twins
5. Gates of Heaven
6. Run, Pung and a Pair
7. Gertie's Garter
10. Wriggly Snake
13. All Pair Honours
15. Heads and Tails (1s and 9s)
16. Chinese Odds
17. Dragonfly (if concealed)
19. Windy Ones (if Pungs concealed)

20. Windy Nines (if Pungs concealed)
21. Greta's Garden
22. Greta's Dragon
23. Sparrow's Sanctuary
24. All Pair Jade
27. All Pair Ruby Jade
28. Ruby Jade
31. Red Lantern (if Pungs from discard)
32. Windy Dragons
33. All Winds and Dragons
34. Three Great Scholars
35. The Four Blessings
36. Dragon's Tail
37. Dragon's Breath
38. Windfall
40. Red Waratah
41. Lillypilly
42. Seven Brothers
43. Three Sisters
44. Green Jade
45. Red Coral
46. White Opal
48. Hachi-Ban

49. Confused Gates
50. Chow Mein
51. Chop Suey
also All Kong and Mixed Pung (see p.30)

Double-Limit

12. Unique Wonder
25. Imperial Jade
26. Lily of the Valley
29. Royal Ruby
30. Red Lily
31. Red Lantern (if concealed)
39. Civil War

Note: 'Concealed' means all tiles from wall except the last which may be claimed from a discard.

Further Variations of Special Hands

36. DRAGON'S TAIL (1st Version)

Score: LIMIT (if concealed)

HALF LIMIT (if exposed)

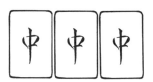 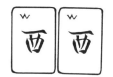

Pung of Dragons.　　Pair of Winds.

Run of 1–9 in any one suit.

DRAGON'S TAIL (2nd Version)

Pair of Dragons.　　Pung of Winds.

Run of 1–9 in any one suit.

37. DRAGON'S BREATH

Score: LIMIT (concealed)

| | Any Dragon tile paired |

One of each Dragon.
Any Dragon paired.
5 Pairs in any one suit.

38. WINDFALL

Score: LIMIT

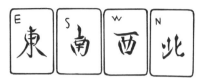

One of each Wind.
5 Pairs of any one suit.

No Dragons.
Concealed (except last tile).

---

39. CIVIL WAR (1861–1865)

Score: DOUBLE LIMIT

Pung of North Winds. Pung of South Winds.
1,8,6,1 in one suit.
1,8,6,5 in another suit.

No Dragons.
Concealed (except last tile).

40. RED WARATAH

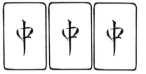 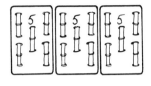 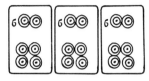 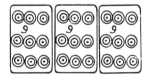 

Pung of Red Dragons.
Pair of Green Dragons.
Pung of Red Bamboos. Pung of Circles. Pung of Characters.

No Winds.

---

41. LILLYPILLY

  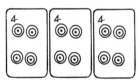 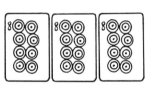

Pung of Green Dragons.
Pair of White Dragons.
3 Pungs of Circles.

No Winds.

42. SEVEN BROTHERS

Score: LIMIT (if all tiles from wall except last)
HALF LIMIT (Pungs from discard)

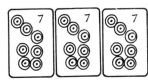   

Pungs or Kongs of 7s in each suit.
One of each Wind.
Any Wind paired.

No Dragons.
Exposed.

---

43. THREE SISTERS

Score: LIMIT (if all tiles from wall except last)
HALF LIMIT (Pungs from discard)

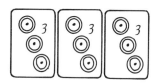 

Pungs or Kongs of 3s in each suit.
One of each Wind.
Any Wind paired.

No Dragons.
Exposed.

44. GREEN JADE

Score: LIMIT

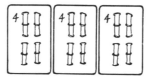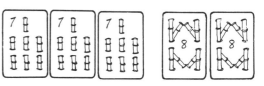

Pung of Green Dragons.
3 Pungs and a Pair of Bamboos.

No Winds.
Exposed.

45. RED CORAL

Score: LIMIT

Pung of Red Dragons.
3 Pungs and a Pair of Characters.

No Winds.
Exposed.

46. WHITE OPAL

Score: LIMIT

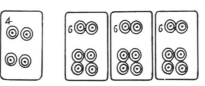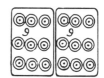

Pung of White Dragons.
3 Pungs and a Pair of Circles.

No Winds.
Exposed.

47. FIVE ODD HONOURS

Score: HALF LIMIT

Five odd Honours, Winds and Dragons. No Pair.
1–9 in any one suit.

Concealed (except last tile).

---

48. HACHI BAN

Score: LIMIT

A sequence of 8 tiles in any one suit (1–8 or 2–9).
Three Pairs of Winds or three Pairs of Dragons.

Concealed (except last tile).

---

49. CONFUSED GATES

Score: LIMIT

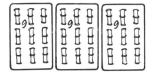

A Pung of 1s in any one suit.
A Pung of 9s in a second suit.
A sequence of 2–8 in a third suit. Any 2–8 paired.

No Winds or Dragons.
Concealed (except last tile).

50. CHOW MEIN

Score: LIMIT

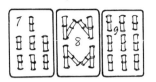 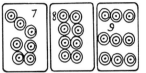 

Chow 7,8,9 in each suit.
One of each Wind.
Any Wind paired.

No Dragons.
Concealed (except last tile).

---

51. CHOP SUEY

Score: LIMIT

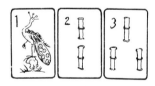 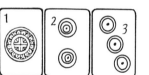  

Chow 1,2,3 in each suit.
One of each Wind.
Any Wind paired.

No Dragons.
Concealed (except last tile).

Two Players

Two-handed Mah Jong is a good game for beginners. They can play in a relaxed atmosphere while learning the rules and gaining confidence with tile combinations. The players are always East Wind and West Wind and sit opposite each other. Four walls are built and procedure is the same as for four players, with East being first to discard.

Rules
1. No Chows are allowed, except in a concealed Mah Jong hand (Buried Treasure) and those in Special hands.
2. The hand must either have a scoring value of at least a half-limit or contain at least four doubles achieved by collecting pungs of tiles with doubling value.
3. East Wind does not pay or receive double.
4. The players pay each other.

Three Players

The wind discs are used to determine playing positions for three-handed Mah Jong but there must always be an East Wind. Four walls are built and play proceeds as for four players. Rule 1 only applies in three handed play. Goulash is played as in the four-handed game but the player opposite the vacant seat selects three tiles from the wall and replaces them with three of his tiles, as do the other players in turn.

Score in the same manner as for four players, but exclude the double for no Chows.

Five Players

As only four people can play at one time, chance dictates which of the five players must sit out a hand. Five tiles are placed face down on the table, four of them being one tile of each wind, the fifth a Dragon tile. The player drawing the Dragon tile sits out for the first hand. Seating positions are decided by the Wind tiles drawn.

Counters are divided between the five players. Play proceeds as for four players. If East Wind loses this hand he retires, the winds move on and the new player takes his place as North Wind. If East Wind wins he remains East Wind and the incoming player waits.

Synopsis of Special Hands

(not including further variations; numbers refer to numbers in illustrations)

Suits only

2. Purity (Three doubles)
Any one suit.
Pungs/Kongs and a Pair
May substitute a Chow for a Pung.

3. Heavenly Twins (Limit)
7 Pairs in any one suit.
Concealed except last tile.

5. Gates of Heaven (Limit)
Pung of 1s in any one suit.
Pung of 9s in same suit.
2–8 in same suit.
Any tile 2–8 paired.

6. Run, Pung and a Pair (Limit)
Run of 1–9 in any one suit.
A Pung and a Pair in same suit.
Concealed except last tile.

7. Gertie's Garter (Limit)
Run of 1–7 in one suit.
Run of 1–7 in another suit.
Concealed except last tile.

8. Knitting (Half limit)
2 suits. 7 Pairs.
Each Pair same number.
Concealed except last tile.

9. Triple Knitting (Half limit)
4 sets and a knitting Pair.
One of each suit of same number.
Concealed except last tile.

15. Heads and Tails (1s and 9s) (Limit)
Pungs/Kongs of 1s and 9s in any suit.
1 Pair of either 1s or 9s.

16. Chinese Odds (Limit)
Any one suit.
Pungs/Kongs and 1 Pair of odd numbers.
Exposed.

23. Sparrow's Sanctuary (Limit)
2 Pairs of 1 Bamboo ('Sparrow's Head').
1 Pair of each Green Bamboo (2,3,4,6,8).
Concealed except last tile.

Winds, Dragons and Suit

1. Ordinary Hand
Any one suit.
4 Pungs/Kongs and 1 Pair.
One Chow may be substituted for one Pung
May include Winds, Dragons or both.

11. Concealed Mah Jong (Buried Treasure)
(2 doubles and extras)
Any one suit.
As many Chows or Pungs as desired.
May include Winds, Dragons or both, and a
Pair.
Every tile from the wall, *including last*.
No Kongs.

All Kong (Limit)
4 Kongs and a Pair in one suit.
May include Winds, Dragons or both.

Mixed Pung (Limit)
4 Pungs and a Pair in any suit.
May include Winds, Dragons or both.
Every tile from the wall *including last*.

Honours

4. All Pair (Half limit)
Any one suit.
7 Pairs, may include Winds, Dragons or both.
Concealed except last tile.

12. Unique Wonder (Double limit)
1s and 9s from each suit.
One of each Wind, one of each Dragon.
Any tile paired.
Concealed except last tile.

13. All Pair Honours (Limit)
Pairs of 1s and 9s in any suit.
May include Winds, Dragons or both.
Concealed except last tile.

14. All Honour Hand (3 doubles plus extras)
Pungs/Kongs of 1s and 9s in any suit, with
Winds, Dragons or both.
A Pair of Honours.
Exposed.

Winds

10. Wriggly Snake (Limit)
Run 1–9 in any one suit.
One of each Wind.
Any tile paired.
Concealed except last tile.

18. **Windy Chow** (Half limit)
One of each Wind with one paired.
1 Chow in each suit.
Concealed except last tile.

19. **Windy Ones** (Limit/half limit)
One of each Wind, any Wind paired.
Pungs/Kongs of 1s in each suit.

20. **Windy Nines** (Limit/half limit)
One of each Wind, any Wind paired.
Pungs/Kongs of 9s in each suit.

35. **Four Blessings** (Limit)
Pungs/Kongs of each Wind.
Pair of anything.
Exposed.

Winds and Dragons

21. **Greta's Garden** (Limit)
Run of 1–7 all in one suit.
One of each Wind.
One of each Dragon.
No Pair.
Concealed except last tile.

22. **Greta's Dragon** (Limit)
Run of 1–7 all in one suit.
One of each Wind.
Pung (not Kong) of Dragons.
Concealed except last tile.

31. **Red Lantern** (Double limit/limit)
Pung/Kong of Red Dragons.
Pung/Kong of Own Wind.
Run from 1–7 in same suit.
Any tile 1–7 paired.

32. **Windy Dragons** (Limit)
One Pair of each Wind.
2 Pungs of any Dragons.
Concealed except last tile.

33. **All Winds and Dragons** (Limit)
Pungs/Kongs of Winds and Dragons only.
Pair of Winds or Dragons.
Exposed.

Dragons

17. **Dragonfly** (Limit/half limit)
One of each Dragon.
Pung/Kong in each of the three suits.
A Pair of any suit.

24. **All Pair Jade** (Limit)
All Pairs of Green Bamboo (2,3,4,6,8).
At least one Pair of Green Dragons.
(2 Pairs do not count as a Kong.)
Concealed except last tile.

25. **Imperial Jade** (Double limit)
Pung or Kong of Green Bamboo (2,3,4,6,8).
Pung of Green Dragons.
One Chow, if desired.
Exposed.

26. **Lily of the Valley** (Double limit)
Pung/Kong of Green Dragons.
Pung/Kong of White Dragons.
2 Pungs/Kong of any Green Bamboo.
1 Pair of Green Bamboo (2,3,4,6,8).
Exposed.

27. **All Pair Ruby Jade** (Limit)
Pair of Red Dragons.
Pair of Green Dragons.
5 Pairs Red and Green Bamboo (1–9).
Concealed except last tile.

28. **Ruby Jade** (Limit)
Pung of Red Dragons.
Pung of Green Dragons.
Pung of Red Bamboo.
Pung of Green Bamboo.
Pair of any Bamboo.
Exposed.

29. **Royal Ruby** (Double limit)
Pung/Kong of Red Dragons.
3 Pungs/Kongs of Red Bamboo (1,5,7,9).
Pair of Red Bamboo.
No Chow.
Exposed.

30. **Red Lily** (Double limit)
Pung/Kong Red Dragons.
Pung/Kong White Dragons.
2 Pungs/Kongs of Red Bamboo (1,5,7,9).
One Pair Red Bamboo.
Exposed.

34. **Three Great Scholars** (Limit)
Pungs/Kongs of all three Dragons.
Pung/Kong or Chow and Pair of any one suit or Winds.
Exposed.

A limit is scored for any hand containing Pungs of all Dragons, or any hand containing Pungs of all Winds.

Limit/Half limit   Limit scored if all tiles come from wall except the last. Half-limit scored if tiles taken from a discard.

Double limit/Limit   Double limit scored if all tiles except the last are taken from the wall. Limit scored if Pungs taken from discards.

Exposed   Pungs made from discards.

Concealed   All tiles from the wall except last which may be taken from a discard.

The Game in Brief

The Set   There are 144 tiles in your set comprising:

3 Suits—Bamboos, Circles and Characters, from 1 to 9; 4 tiles for each (108)
4 Winds—East, South, West and North; 4 tiles for each (16)
3 Dragons—Green, Red and White; 4 tiles for each (12)
8 Seasons (8)

Objective *Western:* To collect four groups, all in the same suit, comprising Pungs, Kongs (one Chow may be substituted for one Pung) and one Pair. Honour tiles may be included. All tiles are used.
Chinese: To collect four groups comprising Pungs, Kongs or Chows (as many as desired) and one Pair. Suits may be mixed. The last 14 tiles are not used. (See page 28.)

Seating   Four players sit at a table and throw two dice in turn.
Highest throw is East and leads the game.
Seating positions as illustrated on page 18.
Place tiles face down and shuffle.

Building the Walls   Four walls are built, 18 tiles long, 2 tiles high, and pushed together to form a square.
East throws two dice to determine (a) whose wall will be opened, and (b) where the break will be.
Counting in an *anti*clockwise direction, start with East as 1 and count until the number thrown is reached. The player who built that wall counts off the same number from the right-hand end of his wall, lifts out these two tiles, places them on top of the wall to the right. These are known as the loose tiles.

The Deal   Starting with East each player takes two pairs (4 tiles) from the left of the opening. East draws first, followed by South, then West, then North and so on until all players have 12 tiles; each player then draws one in turn. East takes one more tile making 14, the other players have 13 tiles. Seasons, if drawn, are placed face up and each player in turn (anticlockwise) takes a replacement tile from the loose tiles. As the two loose tiles are used they are replaced.

Play   East starts by discarding a tile.
A Pung may be formed if any player holds two identical tiles concealed in his hand and the third is discarded. He may pung this tile out of turn, place it in front of him face up and join the two identical tiles to it. This group is now known as an *exposed Pung*. He then discards a tile.
Lost turns   Players between the player discarding the tile and the player who punged the tile lose their turn.
Forming a Chow from a discard   If the tile is not claimed for a Pung, the player on the right of the discarder may claim it for a Chow (providing he has the other two tiles forming the chow concealed in his hand). No other player may claim this tile for a Chow unless it allows him to complete his hand. If the tile is not claimed, the player on the right of the discarder draws the next tile from the wall at the open end, places it in his hand, hidden from the other players, then discards a tile.
An exposed Kong   An exposed Pung cannot be made into an exposed Kong from a discard; it may be converted with an identical tile drawn from the wall. A loose tile must be taken for a Kong or the number of tiles in the hand will be short; it is taken before discarding.

A concealed Kong should be placed on the table and a loose tile taken.

Seasons and Flowers act as bonus tiles, taking no part in the play. They must be exposed and a loose tile taken as a replacement.

Pair Only the winning hand may claim a tile to form a pair.

Drawn game If no player has gone Mah Jong before the last 14 tiles (Chinese game) or all the tiles (Western version) have been taken, the game is said to be drawn. All the tiles are reshuffled, the walls rebuilt, East remains East and continues as East if he wins in the Chinese game. In the Western version East remains East for only one more hand and a Goulash is played.

Winning There must be at least 14 tiles in a winning combination. The winner displays 14 tiles and makes no discard.

Payment The three losing players pay the winner, who pays no-one. East pays or receives double. The other players total their scores and pay each other the differences.

If East wind wins he remains East. If East loses, the next player on the right becomes the new East Wind and all players change winds.

Calling or Fishing A player needing one tile to go Mah Jong may take it from any discard. He has precedence over all other players.

Penalties A player with too few tiles may not correct this; he may score, but cannot go Mah Jong. A player with too many tiles pays all other players, scores nothing, and cannot go Mah Jong.

Tournament Play

The following suggestions might help players when organising tournaments.

1. Jokers, Season and Flower tiles are removed.

2. Four-handed version only is played.

3. Goulash is not played after a drawn game.

4. East passes on at the end of each hand. This reduces the element of luck and gives all players an equal chance. A round therefore is limited to four hands.

5. The limit is set at 1000 points.

6. Before play commences, rules to be used should be established.

7. If Special hands are used, not more than fourteen hands, offering the greatest range, should be selected. This will simplify the supervision of the scoring.

8. No player may go Mah Jong with the same Special Hand for more than two consecutive turns.

Bibliography

Anon: *Standard Rules for the Chinese Domino Game of Mah Jong*, Nanjing.
Babcock, Joseph: *Babcock's Rules for Mah Jongg*, Shanghai, 1923.
Bray, Jean: *How to Play Mah Jong*, New York, 1924.
Foster, R.F.: *Foster on Mah Jong*, New York, 1924.
Headley, G. and Seeley, Y.: *Mah Jong, K.T.G.* (Know the Game), London, 1978.
Millington, A.D.: *Complete Book of Mah Jong*, London, 1977.
Robertson, Max: *The Game of Mah Jong*, Whitcoulls, Auckland, 1974.
Strauser, K. and Evans, L.: *Mah Jong, Anyone?*, C. Tuttle, Japan, 1964.
Walters, D.: *Your Future Revealed by the Mah Jongg*, Northamptonshire, 1982.

Index

Seating Indicator

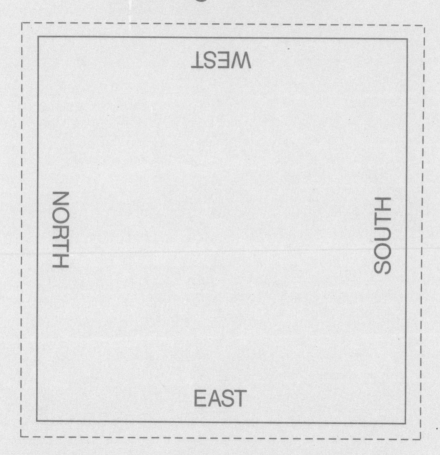

Cut along the dotted line to obtain your seating indicator. Place it on the table, and when the East Wind moves anticlockwise, rotate the indicator to correspond.